creatures
of the sea

# The
# Walrus

**Other titles in the series:**

creatures of the sea

# The
# Walrus

**Kris Hirschmann**

KIDHAVEN
PRESS™

San Diego • Detroit • New York • San Francisco • Cleveland
New Haven, Conn. • Waterville, Maine • London • Munich

© 2003 by KidHaven Press. KidHaven Press is an imprint of The Gale Group, Inc., a division of Thomson Learning, Inc.

KidHaven™ and Thomson Learning™ are trademarks used herein under license.

*For more information, contact*
KidHaven Press
27500 Drake Rd.
Farmington Hills, MI 48331-3535
Or you can visit our Internet site at http://www.gale.com

LIBRARY OF CONGRESS CATALOGING-IN-PUBLICATION DATA

Hirschmann, Kris, 1967-
The walrus / by Kristine Hirschmann.
v. cm. — (Creatures of the sea)
Includes bibliographical references and index.
Contents: The whale-horse — Walrus homes and habits — The hunter and the hunted — From birth to death.
ISBN 0-7377-1557-X (hardback : alk. paper)
1. Walrus—Juvenile literature. [1. Walrus.] I. Title.
QL737.P62 H57 2004 599.79'9—dc21

2002154428

Printed in China

# Table of Contents

# Mighty Marine Mammals

Walruses are among the most massive animals on Earth. On land, they are also among the most awkward. A walrus out of the water heaves its enormous body from place to place with great effort and little grace. To an observer, it may seem surprising that such a clumsy animal manages to survive.

In the ocean, however, everything is different. With its bulk supported by the water, a walrus is a sleek and skillful swimmer. It twists and turns smoothly as it hunts, travels, plays, and mates. The walrus's grace in the water shows that although this animal spends much of its time on land, it is truly a creature of the sea.

Indeed, walruses belong to a group of animals called **marine mammals**. Marine mammals are animals that breathe air, are warm-blooded, and have other mammalian traits, yet live in an ocean environment. To be classified as a marine mammal,

*An adult walrus swims through icy water.*

an animal does not have to spend all its time in the water. It does, however, have to live near the sea and depend on the water to meet some of its needs. Walruses need the ocean for food and many other things. And even when on land, they never stray far from the water's edge. So walruses definitely earn the right to be called marine mammals.

Walruses live in places where the climate is uncomfortably cold for most people and spend most of their time in remote places that are difficult for people to reach. For these reasons, it can be hard for scientists to study walruses in the wild. In the past few decades, however, some scientific organizations have captured young walruses and taken them to live in marine parks and zoos. Captive walruses allow scientists to learn more about walrus behavior and biology. They also educate the public about walrus habits and lifestyles. Thanks to today's zoos and aquariums, people who would never get the chance to see a walrus in the wild can get a firsthand look at these mighty marine mammals.

# The Whale-Horse

The word "walrus" comes from an old Scandinavian word, *hvalros* or *valroos*, which means "whale-horse." It is likely that this word dates back to the Vikings, a seagoing people who traveled the world's northern oceans and probably saw many walruses during their journeys.

A walrus does not look like either a whale or a horse, but it is not hard to see why the Vikings gave the walrus this name. Like whales and horses, walruses are large, powerful creatures that are completely at home in their native environment. With their enormous bodies and strong limbs, walruses dominate any area in which they appear.

There are two types of walruses: the Pacific walrus and the Atlantic walrus. Although both types of

*The Pacific walrus, shown here, is larger and heavier than the Atlantic walrus.*

walrus are large, the Pacific variety outweighs its Atlantic relatives. Adult male Pacific walruses weigh between eighteen hundred and thirty-eight hundred pounds and measure 9 to 12 feet in length; females weigh between nine hundred and twenty-eight hundred pounds and measure 7 ½ to 10 feet in length. Male and female Atlantic walruses tend to weigh just a little bit less than their Pacific relatives, and their length is quite a bit shorter. Atlantic males grow only up to 9 ½ feet, and females are not usually longer than 8 feet.

All walruses' bodies are plump and rounded. The head is small compared to the rest of the walrus, and it is attached to the body without any visible neck. A large midsection tapers into two large forelimbs (at the front of the body) and two smaller hindlimbs (at the rear).

All four of the walrus's limbs are shaped like flippers. Because of this trait, walruses are known as **pinnipeds**, which comes from Latin words meaning "fin-footed." (Seals and sea lions, the walrus's closest relatives, are also part of the pinniped group.) On land, the walrus arranges its strong limbs underneath its body and uses them to walk. In the ocean, the walrus uses its hindflippers to push itself through the water. The foreflippers are held close to the body and used to help the walrus steer.

Adult walruses are cinnamon brown in color and have tough, wrinkled skin. In males, the skin is bunched into large lumps called **tubercles**. The skin of both males and females is covered with a thin coat of hair, which is shed once a year in a process called **molting**. Males usually molt from June through August. Females also molt around this time but often take longer to lose their hair than males do.

## Ivory Tusks

One of the walrus's most distinctive features is its two long tusks. These long front teeth are made of a hard material called ivory. They begin to grow during a young walrus's first summer or fall and continue to grow for about fifteen years.

Both males and females have tusks, but the tusks look slightly different depending on the sex of the walrus. Males' tusks tend to be longer. They grow to a maximum length of nearly forty inches, while females' tusks are not usually longer than about thirty inches. Also, males' tusks are normally thicker and straighter than females' tusks.

Walruses have many uses for their tusks. The tusks can be deadly weapons when used to jab predators or other walruses. Tusks also affect a walrus's social status; individuals with longer tusks are usually dominant in the herd. Tusks may also be used to chop holes in ice and to pull the body out of the water and onto large, floating slabs of ice called ice floes. The walrus's scientific family name, *Odobenidae*, comes from this last usage. In Greek, *Odobenidae* means "tooth walkers."

A walrus's tusks reach their maximum length when a walrus is about ten years old. After that time, the tusks begin to wear down from constant use. They may also break off. For these reasons, older walruses often have shortened or missing tusks.

## Built for the Cold

Like all mammals, walruses are warm-blooded. This means they maintain a steady internal temperature.

*Because of their flipper-like limbs, walruses are part of a group of aquatic mammals known as pinnipeds.*

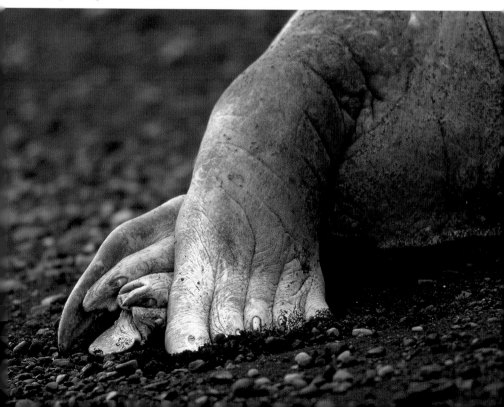

Regardless of the temperature of the surrounding air or water, a walrus's core temperature is always about ninety-eight degrees Fahrenheit. Yet these

*A walrus uses its long tusks to pull itself out of the water.*

warm-blooded animals live in extremely cold climates. During the winter, water temperatures in a walrus's home environment are usually close to the freezing point, and air temperatures may be much lower. Walruses' bodies are specially designed to keep warm in these extreme conditions.

## Thick-Skinned

The walrus's skin provides the first layer of protection. The skin is tough and leathery and may be as much as one and one-half inches thick in places. This thick skin not only provides a barrier against the cold, it is also full of small blood vessels that constrict, or get narrower, in chilly conditions. Less blood flows through constricted vessels, which means that less body heat reaches the surface of the skin. The heat stays deep inside the walrus's body where it cannot be whisked away by cold air or water.

If a walrus spends a lot of time in very cold water, the vessels in its skin may constrict so much that almost no blood reaches the skin's surface. When this happens, the walrus's usual cinnamon-brown color disappears, and the walrus becomes almost white. After the walrus spends some time out of the water, though, the blood vessels in the skin open up and the walrus gets its normal color back.

Thick skin is not the walrus's only protection from the cold. Walruses also have a layer of body fat called **blubber** that lies just underneath the skin. Blubber is an excellent insulator that keeps a walrus's body heat from escaping. In a large walrus, the blubber layer may be nearly four inches thick in some places.

## Sensing the World

Walruses find their way around their chilly homes with the help of many senses. Hearing, smell, and touch are especially important to the walrus.

Although walruses have no external ears, they seem to have excellent hearing. Scientists believe that walruses hear best underwater. However, walruses also hear quite well on land. People imitating walrus sounds have gotten responses from walruses more than a mile away, and walruses have been seen fleeing when they hear predators approaching. Hearing is also important in a social sense. Walruses communicate with each other through a variety of sounds, including bellows, tooth-clacking, whistles, and more.

The walrus's sense of smell is very good as well. Walruses smell through two small nostrils found on the snout. Walruses seem to recognize each other mostly by scent, with mother walruses in particular using this sense to identify their babies. Smell is also used to detect predators.

Touch is another important sense for the walrus. A walrus's thick skin does not feel much, but its snout is another story. Walruses' snouts bear

*Walruses have a highly developed sense of smell. They use their noses and their sensitive whiskers to find food underwater.*

between four hundred and seven hundred whiskers called **vibrissae** that are extremely sensitive to touch. If anything brushes against the vibrissae, electrical signals are sent to the walrus's brain. The brain receives these signals and reads them to discover what caused the disturbance. Signals from the vibrissae are especially useful in dark underwater areas, where it is hard for the walrus to see.

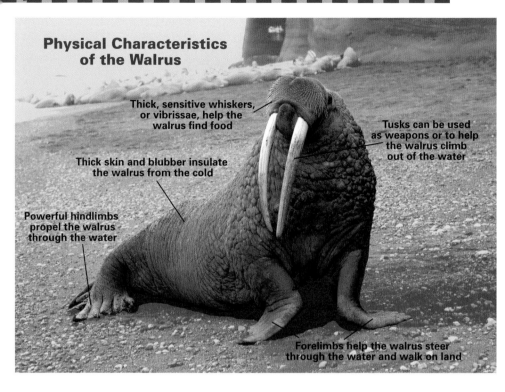

**Physical Characteristics of the Walrus**

Thick, sensitive whiskers, or vibrissae, help the walrus find food

Tusks can be used as weapons or to help the walrus climb out of the water

Thick skin and blubber insulate the walrus from the cold

Powerful hindlimbs propel the walrus through the water

Forelimbs help the walrus steer through the water and walk on land

A walrus cannot see well out of the water either. Walruses' eyes are small and not as sharp as those of the other pinnipeds. So a walrus probably does not depend on this sense as much as it does on its senses of hearing, smell, and touch. But poor eyesight is no problem for the walrus, which has everything it needs to succeed in its home environment.

# chapter 2

# Walrus Homes and Habits

Walruses are found only in the earth's northern regions. Atlantic walruses live in the Atlantic and Arctic Oceans, mostly along the coasts of Greenland and northeastern Canada. Pacific walruses live in shallow areas of the Bering, Chukchi, and Laptev Seas, parts of the Pacific and Arctic Oceans found between Russia and Alaska. The home ranges of Atlantic and Pacific walruses do not overlap, so the two populations never meet.

There are about fifty thousand Atlantic walruses and two hundred thousand Pacific walruses in the world. There is evidence that the Pacific walrus population is about as big as it can get based on the amount of resources available. The Atlantic walrus population, though, still has room to grow.

*A small group of walruses rests on a small ice floe. Walruses prefer the frigid water of the Arctic region.*

## Life in the Herd

Walruses are social animals. They live in herds of hundreds or even thousands of individuals. Adult males and females form separate herds.

Within each herd, there is a clear social order. A walrus's place in the herd society is determined mostly by size, tusks, and aggressiveness. Large, pushy walruses with long tusks have the highest social ranking. These walruses get the best resting spots. When it is time to mate, they also tend to attract the biggest, strongest partners.

To assert itself and get what it wants, a walrus usually rears its head back and points its tusks at another walrus. It may also roar or make other loud noises. Usually these displays convince a weaker walrus to get out of the way. If the other walrus does not back down, a fight may occur. Fighting walruses slash at each other with their tusks, sometimes doing serious damage. They may give each other long, bleeding cuts or even puncture each other's skin and flesh. Fighting is most common among male walruses, most of which bear scars on their necks, chests, and shoulders from past battles.

Aside from the occasional fight, though, walruses get along well. Most of the time, thousands of walruses can share the same resting and hunting spots without conflict.

## A Good Home

As marine mammals, walruses spend most of their time in the water. Scientists estimate that at least two-thirds of a walrus's life is spent swimming in the ocean. The rest of the time is spent out of the water on land or on ice. The process by which a walrus leaves the water is called **hauling out**. Any place where herds of walruses gather out of the water is called a **haulout**.

Whenever possible, walruses haul out on large, free-floating slabs of ice. They prefer new ice, which is not as thick or as hard as older ice. Walruses sometimes make holes in ice to get to the water, and new ice is easier for the walrus to break with its tusks or its hard head. Walruses also prefer areas where the ice sheet is broken up into chunks rather than frozen into one large surface. Floating ice slabs with a surface area between one thousand and two thousand square feet are especially popular. A slab of this size is large enough to be stable,

*Male walruses point their tusks at each other to establish their position in the herd.*

but small enough to provide easy access to the water on all sides.

Although walruses prefer to haul out on ice, they will rest on land if no ice is available. Quiet beaches and small, rocky islands are favorite spots. Walrus herds tend to come back to the same land haulouts year after year. Round Island off the southwestern coast of Alaska and the King, St. Lawrence, and Punuk Islands in the Chukchi Sea are a few of the places where walruses are known to gather.

Whether they haul out on land or on ice, walruses like places where the weather is consistently cold. Walruses are most comfortable in air temperatures ranging from about five to forty degrees Fahrenheit, and they are used to swimming in ice-cold water.

## Migration

Because walruses enjoy cold weather and ice, most migrate with the seasons. They probably do not migrate on purpose, as many animals do. Instead, they simply stay near the edges of the Arctic ice pack, the frozen sea surrounding the North Pole, which gets bigger and smaller depending on the time of year. During the wintertime the ice pack is at its largest, so walruses are pushed to the southernmost area of their home range. During the summertime, when much of the ice pack melts, the same walruses may be found thousands of miles to the north.

*Once they are out of the water, walruses love to huddle together.*

Scientists have carefully tracked the migration routes of Pacific walruses. They have discovered that in the winter, the entire Pacific walrus population is found in the Bering Sea. The walruses stay there until the ice pack begins to break up in the spring, when they start moving north. From May through June, most Pacific walruses pass through the Bering Strait into the Chukchi Sea. They keep moving northward through the Chukchi Sea as the ice pack continues to melt. In late September, however, the ice pack begins to grow again as the weather gets colder. This is the walruses' signal to start moving south for the winter.

Pacific females and young walruses make the longest migrations. Males do not usually travel as far from season to season. One group of several thousand male Pacific walruses even stays in the Bering Sea all year round, hauling out on land instead of pack ice.

The migration habits of Atlantic walruses have not been studied in detail. However, scientists believe that Atlantic walruses also make north/south migrations but do not travel nearly as far as Pacific walruses.

## Walruses at Rest

Even during a walrus's long migration, there is plenty of time to rest—a favorite walrus activity. When it is time to rest, a walrus usually hauls out of the water. To do this, it may simply climb onto ice or land. Other times, though, a walrus may sink its tusks into an icy surface, using them as anchors to help pull its bulk out of the water.

After leaving the ocean, resting walruses huddle together in groups. They huddle partly because skin-to-skin contact helps them hold onto their body heat when the weather is cold. But even when the weather is warm, walruses like to stay close to other walruses. Sometimes hundreds of walruses can be seen lounging in huge piles. The walruses lie in every imaginable position—on their stomachs, their sides, their backs, and even on top of other walruses.

Although walruses prefer to climb out of the water when it is time to relax, they can rest in the water if necessary. A walrus can attach itself to a floating chunk of ice by sinking its tusks into the edge of the ice. The anchored walrus can then go to sleep and travel along with the ice floe. Walruses can also make their bodies float by sucking air into special sacs in their necks. After the sacs are inflated, the walrus floats effortlessly with its head out of the water. A walrus can easily sleep in this position, letting its body drift with the ocean currents. These unusual resting techniques are well suited to one of the world's most unusual animals.

# 3

# The Hunter and the Hunted

Walruses are **carnivores**. This means they eat the flesh of other animals. Most of the animals on which walruses feed are sea creatures that live below the ocean's surface, so hunting and eating take place in the water. In this environment, walruses are skilled hunters that have no trouble getting the food they need to survive.

## Walrus Meals

With their big bodies, walruses are big eaters. Adult walruses eat between 4 and 6 percent of their own body weight each day. A big male walrus may eat well over two hundred pounds of food in a twenty-four-hour period.

A walrus's diet consists mostly of small, bottom-dwelling mollusks (soft-bodied animals with hard shells). Clams, one type of mollusk, are most walruses' favorite food. Walruses may also eat crustaceans (animals with external skeletons, such as shrimp and crabs), worms, sea cucumbers, and other creatures that are found on the ocean floor. Fish are not usually eaten.

Very rarely, a walrus develops a taste for seal flesh. Once a walrus decides it likes seals, it eats little else. Seal-eating walruses are usually larger and stronger than other walruses. Seal eaters can also be recognized by the greasy stains on their skin and tusks. These stains are left by the seals' blubber.

When it is ready to eat, a walrus leaves its resting place and plunges into the ocean. Once in the water, the walrus searches for food through a series of foraging dives. Foraging dives average about seven minutes in length and are separated by rest periods of one to two minutes. The walrus makes as many dives as necessary to fill its stomach.

## Finding Food

Because walruses eat mostly bottom-dwelling animals, they tend to make their foraging dives in areas where the water is not too deep and the bottom is reached easily. Most feeding takes place at depths between 30 and 150 feet. Walruses may dive as deep as 300 feet to search for food if they happen to be in a deep spot or if no food is available in shallow waters. Such deep dives, however, are rare.

*Walruses must dive to find their food along the ocean floor.*

To find food, a walrus swims down and presses its snout against the ocean floor. The walrus then uses its powerful hindflippers to push itself forward. As the walrus travels, it roots through the bottom sand and sediment with its snout. It uses its sensitive vibrissae to feel its way and to detect prey.

Once a walrus finds a meal, it must get the animal into its mouth. If the animal is not buried, the walrus simply takes hold of it by biting. Animals that are covered with sand or silt, however, must be uncovered first. To reach buried prey, a walrus sucks in a mouthful of water, then blows a strong stream at the sea floor. The stream of water blasts away any loose material covering the prey. Once the prey has been uncovered, the walrus can seize it.

Walruses do not chew their prey. They swallow it whole. Soft-bodied or thin-shelled animals are gulped down immediately. Clams and other bivalves (animals that have hinged shells) are sucked out of their thick, protective shells before being eaten.

## Natural Enemies

When a walrus is out hunting, it does not have to worry much about being attacked by other predators. Walruses are so large that they are safe from most of the animals in the sea. But there are two creatures that can and do attack walruses occasionally. These two creatures are the polar bear and the killer whale. Both predators will eat young or weak walruses if they get the chance.

Even polar bears and killer whales, however, stay away from healthy, fully grown walruses. Adult walruses are not only big, they are also fierce and strong, and their tusks make dangerous weapons. Walruses can kill polar bears by holding them with their front flippers, then stabbing them with their tusks. And dead killer whales have been found with walrus tusks embedded in their flesh. No one can say for sure whether the walruses' stabs killed the whales, but the wounds were certainly painful.

## Walrus versus Human

The walrus's size, strength, and natural weapons cannot keep it safe from the most dangerous predators of all: humans. People kill thousands of walruses each year for the animals' blubber oil, tusk ivory, skins, and more.

The history of walrus hunting by humans is a long one. There is evidence that the earliest native peoples of the north killed walruses and used their body parts for meat, fuel oil, tools, and many other necessities. Around the ninth century, people also

*Polar bears and killer whales are natural enemies of the walrus.*

began to hunt walruses commercially, mostly to harvest the animals' valuable ivory tusks. Ever larger numbers of walruses were killed over the centuries until the population began to shrink dangerously. Between the mid-1800s and 1960, walruses nearly became extinct three times as the result of overhunting.

Today, laws protect walruses from most hunters. In the United States, the Walrus Act of 1941 and the Marine Mammal Protection Act of 1972 make it illegal for commercial operators to kill walruses. The Canadian and Russian governments also have

*A Chukchi hunter stands near walrus hides stretched out to dry in the sun. Like other native peoples of the Arctic, the Chukchi are allowed to hunt walruses.*

laws that govern the hunting of walruses. And in 1975, the Pacific walrus gained international protection when it was placed on Appendix III of the Convention on International Trade in Endangered Species (CITES). Animals on Appendix III are not endangered. However, they are protected in at least one country, and the protecting country has asked other countries to help keep an eye on the animal in question. When many countries cooperate, it is less likely for illegal hunting to go unnoticed.

All countries where walruses live do allow limited walrus hunting by native groups. This is because the walrus is an important part of many native tribes' heritage, and walrus hunting helps these tribes to keep their traditions alive. An estimated six thousand walruses are killed legally each year by native hunters around the world.

Native hunters do not kill enough walruses to threaten the population, however. Plenty of walruses are born each year to take the place of those that lose their lives. Under current conditions, both the Atlantic and Pacific walrus populations should thrive far into the future.

# chapter 21

# From Birth to Death

Walruses have fairly long lives. If a walrus does not get sick or injured, it can expect to live about thirty years. A few walruses live even longer. A particularly healthy walrus may live to be forty years old.

During its lifetime, a walrus moves through a cycle that includes birth, development, adulthood, and parenthood. This cycle produces new walruses and keeps populations steady.

## The Newborn Walrus

Baby walruses are called calves. Calves are born sometime between April and June, during the adult walruses' northward migration. A pregnant female hauls out onto an ice floe to give birth, usually to a single **calf**. Twins are born every now and then, but they are rare.

Walrus calves are big. Newborn walruses usually weigh between 100 and 165 pounds and measure between three and four feet in length. They are dark gray in color and are covered with a coat of soft, short fur. This fur turns brown within a couple of weeks. After one or two months, the newborn's fur falls off and is replaced by adult hair. The calf is still darker than adult walruses, however. The young walrus will get lighter over time, reaching its adult color several years after it is born.

Walrus calves are fairly strong and are able to swim as soon as they are born. However, a newborn

*A walrus calf floats next to its mother.*

calf does not have enough blubber to keep it warm in the cold water, so it usually stays out of the ocean for several weeks after its birth. Even in the air, a young walrus may feel chilly. When this happens, it often snuggles up to its mother to stay warm.

A newborn walrus has another reason to stay close to its mother. It is too small and weak to defend itself from predators, so it needs its mother's constant protection. Adult females carefully guard their calves and often cradle them between their foreflippers. A mother walrus may even shelter a calf under her massive chest to keep it hidden and safe. And if a mother walrus must leave her baby to hunt, other walruses will look after the baby until she returns.

## The Early Years

Like all mammals, walruses produce milk for their babies. Calves drink their mothers' milk by nursing from nipples on the underside of the body. They may nurse in the water, on ice, or on land. Calves usually nurse for the first six months of their lives. After six months they may begin eating some solid food in addition to their mother's milk. However, most calves get at least some of their food through nursing until they are nearly two years old.

A calf and its mother live together as long as nursing continues. Usually the nursing period lasts about two years, or until the mother is preparing to give birth to another calf. At that point the young

*An adult and baby walrus snuggle together on Round Island, Alaska.*

walrus leaves its mother and starts to take care of itself. A young male will stay with its mother's herd for another two or three years and then leave to join an adult all-male herd. A female will stay with its mother's herd for the rest of its life.

After leaving its mother's side, a young walrus switches to a grown-up diet of clams and other sea creatures. Over time it continues to get larger and stronger. It also matures, gradually turning into an adult. Female walruses are considered to be young adults when they reach five to six years of age. Males mature more slowly, reaching adulthood somewhere between eight and ten years of age.

## Mating Season

Once a walrus becomes an adult, it is able to have calves of its own. Few walruses, however, reproduce as soon as they reach maturity. Females usually have their first calf when they are about ten years old. Males do not usually reproduce until about fifteen years of age, when they finally become big and strong enough to attract mates.

For walruses, mating season takes place between December and March. During this period, adult female walruses who are not pregnant come into **estrus** (readiness to mate) and seek male herds. The males respond by competing for the females' attention. They do this mostly by swimming around the females and making a variety of noises. Bell-like sounds, whistles, and clacking are all part of the males' display. Males may also fight with each other at this time. The competition for mates becomes fierce as older, stronger walruses try to drive younger and weaker walruses away from the female herd.

When a female becomes interested in a male, she joins him in the water and swims away from the rest of the herd. The pair then mates in the water. With a little luck, the mating will cause the female to become pregnant.

By the end of the mating season, most of the females who were in estrus will be pregnant. The male and female herds break apart, going their separate ways for another year.

## Carrying the Baby

A baby walrus starts out as a tiny fertilized egg deep inside the mother walrus's uterus. This fertilized egg does not start growing immediately. It floats in the uterus for four to five months before attaching to the uterus wall and starting to develop. After the

*During mating season, male walruses compete for attention.*

egg begins to develop, it takes another eleven months for the calf to be born. A female walrus therefore is pregnant for fifteen to sixteen months with each calf.

Because the walrus's pregnancy is longer than a year, pregnant females skip the following year's mating season. They give birth a few months after mating season ends and then must wait until the next winter to mate again. This means that a female walrus can give birth no more than once every two years. Young females in their prime often

*Though it may be hard for most people to see walruses in their Arctic habitat, the creatures are popular attractions at zoos.*

stick to this schedule, calving every other year. Older females tend to be less fertile and give birth less often.

At the end of a walrus's long pregnancy, a new calf is born. The calf is young and helpless, just like its parents were when they came into the world. But the calf grows quickly, gaining up to two pounds each day and growing between four and six inches in length each month. Before long the calf will be a young adult. It will be ready to have babies of its own, and the cycle of life will continue.

# Glossary

**blubber:** A thick layer of fat that lies just beneath the walrus's skin.

**calf:** A baby walrus.

**carnivore:** Any animal that eats the flesh of other animals to survive.

**estrus:** Readiness to mate.

**hauling out:** The process by which a walrus leaves the water.

**haulout:** Any place where walruses gather out of the water.

**marine mammal:** A mammal that lives in an ocean environment.

**molting:** The annual shedding of hair.

**pinniped:** Any of a group of "fin-footed" mammals, including seals, sea lions, and walruses.

**tubercles:** Large lumps on an adult male walrus's skin.

**vibrissae:** Touch-sensitive whiskers found on the walrus's snout.

# For Further Exploration

## Books

Kathy Darling, *Walrus: On Location*. New York: Lothrop, Lee & Shepard, 1991. This book includes good general information about walruses, plus some stories of interesting walrus behavior observed firsthand by the author.

David Miller, *Seals and Sea Lions*. Stillwater, MN: Voyageur Press, 1998. Read about the walrus's closest cousins in this book. Many beautiful photographs illustrate the informative text.

Barbara Taylor, *Arctic & Antarctic*. New York: Random House, 1995. This book includes fabulous photographs plus informative text about life at the earth's poles. Walruses, penguins, caribou, moose, and other animals are highlighted.

## Internet Sources

*Public Broadcasting Service*, "Toothwalkers." www.pbs.org. Follow the links on this page for information about walruses in captivity and the dangers of filming walruses in the wild.

*U.S. Department of the Interior*, "Pacific Walrus Research Just For Kids!!" www.absc.usgs.gov. This website has lots of good information about walruses, written just for kids.

## Video

Adam Raveth, *Toothwalkers: Giants of the Arctic Ice.* A Sarah Robertson and Great North production in association with Thirteen WNET, Discovery Channel Canada, Docstar and Canal B, 1997. This amazing documentary contains the first underwater footage ever shot of wild walruses.

# Index

# picture credits

# about the author

Kris Hirschmann has written more than seventy books for children. She is the president of The Wordshop, a business that provides a wide variety of writing and editorial services. She holds a bachelor's degree in psychology from Dartmouth College in Hanover, New Hampshire. Hirschmann lives just outside of Orlando, Florida, with her husband, Michael, and her daughter, Nikki.